ISAAC GIWA

ACHIEVING

OUTSTANDING

BUSINESS

SUCCESS

POWERFUL KEYS FOR A BUSINESS OF EXCELLENCE AND GREATNESS

ISAAC GIWA

ACHIEVING OUTSTANDING BUSINESS SUCCESS

Copyright © 2017 by ISAAC **GIWA**

All rights reserved

No part of this publication may be reproduced or transmitted in whole in any form or by any means, electronic or mechanical, including photocopying, recording, or by any information storage and retrieval system, without the written permission of the publisher.

Published by

ISGIBSON SERVICES

6, kamoru Adeyemi Street, Ire-Akari Estate, Isolo, Lagos-Nigeria.

P.O. Box 621, Ikeja

Lagos, Nigeria

Tel: 234-1-8023147715

234-1-8036665662

E-mail: isgibsonservices@gmail.com

isaacgiwabooks@gmail.com

NB: All scripture quotations are from the King James Version of the Bible, except otherwise stated.

Contents

1. 3

PASSION! KEY TO GREAT ACHIEVEMENT..3

    SECRET OF OUTSTANDING SUCCESS............4

    ACT AND PROSPER..4

2. 6

THE POWER OF PREPARATION.................6

    MAXIMUM EFFECTIVENESS..........................7

    FACT FINDING..7

3 8

BE ADDICTED TO ACQUIRING RELEVANT INFORMATION 8

21ST CENTURY BUSINESS 9

MEET THE MOST RECOGNIZABLE ENTREPRENEUR IN THE U.K 9

MARY KAY'S SECRET 10

HOW TO GENERATE BUSINESS IDEA 11

THREE WAYS OF ACQUIRING INFORMATION 11

4 13

PERSONAL RESPONSIBILITY.................13

7 KEYS TO PERSONAL RESPONSIBILITY.......13

5...15

PERSONAL DEVELOPMENT....................15

BE A SUPER ACHIEVER................................15

NEW WAYS..16

MENTAL DEVELOPMENT..............................16

LIVE HEALTHY..17

WORK ON YOUR APPEARANCE....................17

6..18

HANDLING BUSINESS PRESSURE...........18

GREAT OPPORTUNITIES INSIDE OPPOSITION..18

STRATEGIES IN HANDLING BUSINESS PRESSURE...19

7..21

COMMITMENT TO DUTY...........................21

BE ON MOTION..22

8..24

DEVELOP YOUR MIND POWER.................24

BE AN ACHIEVER..24

THINK SOLUTION...25

NOT YOUR COLOUR..25

THINK BIG..26

9..27

STRESS MANAGEMENT..................................27

PRINCIPLE GUARANTEEING A STRESS-FREE LIFE..28

10..29

BUILD A BUSINESS TEAM ALLIANCE.....29

WHAT IS A BUSINESS TEAM ALLIANCE?......29

INVOLVE OTHERS..29

BENEFITS OF BUILDING A TEAM ALLIANCE..30

HOW TO MAKE A BUSINESS TEAM ALLIANCE WORK..31

OTHER BOOKS BY ISAAC GIWA...............33

GET CONNECTED..37

OUR MISSION..38

YOUR LETTER IS VERY IMPORTANT TO ME..39

WILL YOU BECOME A PARTNER WITH MY MINISTRY?..............................40

BOOK ENCOUNTERS................................41

1

PASSION! KEY TO GREAT ACHIEVEMENT

You can have anything you want if you want it desperately enough. You must want it with an inner exuberance that erupts the skin and joins the energy that created the world. — Sheila Graham

Business success is for the hungry. For you to be successful in business life, you must have a passion.

Passion is to crave or long for something with intensity. To become successful entrepreneur, you must have a burning desire to accumulate wealth. A mild desire or casual interest is not enough.

Passion is an essential requirement for business success. It is burning desire to be special and do something extraordinary with your life. Keep this in mind, feeble desire brings feeble results, just as a small amount of fire makes a small amount of heat.

It was the passion of being a world recognized scientist that drove Albert Einstein and Isaac Newton and all those acknowledge scientist to persist and persevere in their researches and theories until a breakthrough was found. It was the passion of being the greatest inventor in America that drove Thomas Edison to spend long months before he could perfect incandescent electric lamp and despite the fact that he failed more than 10,000 times, that passion carried him to the discovery for which he was searching. Passion is what keep an entrepreneur going when the going gets tough.

You must move towards the achievement of your business dream. Let it become an obsession. Put everything you've got inside that dream, that's when result will begin to come.

SECRET OF OUTSTANDING SUCCESS.

"Never consent to creep when you feel an impulse to soar". – Helen Keller.

Nothing can stop a man with a passion. They tried to stop Nelson Mandela but because of his passion, he won. He was imprisoned for 27 years in the process of trying to secure independence for his nation – and freedom from colonial oppression.

He eventually won the independence for his country and returned from prison to become the first black president of the nation of South Africa. The secret to the outstanding success of Dr Mandela was that he was passionate and ready to pay the price to accomplish his goal.

Passion means you'll move forward even in the face of opposition

Passion means in disappointment, you still move forward.

Passion means in criticism, you sill move forward.

Passion means that you have found something not only to live for but to die for.

"The longer I live, the more I am certain that the great difference between men, between the feeble and the powerful, between the great and the insignificant is energy, invincible determination, a purpose once fixed, and then

death or victory – Sir Thomas Fowel Buxton.

ACT AND PROSPER

Business is not being in traction, it is being in ACTION. Nothing moves, until you move it. It is not to just have a strong desire; you must always act on it. Passion without action is only a wish. Once you are aware of the business dream that has been birthed in your heart, there comes a time when you must prove that you desire what dream has been birthed in your heart by acting on it. Mike Murdock says, "The proof of desire is pursuit".

What you are not willing to pursue, you don't respect and what you don't respect, you will never attract. Therefore, you need to turn your passion loose by doing something about it; something practical and positive.

Don't wait for a perfect condition because a perfect condition may never come. start doing something about your life passion now.

A strong passion for any object will ensure success, for the desire of the end will point out the means – William Hazlitt.

2

THE POWER OF PREPARATION

> **Spectular achievements come from spectacular preparation. – Roger Staubach**

An unprepared field will make a frustrated farmer. Preparation is the guarantee for your desired business success. What you don't prepared for, you cannot successfully partake of. Business pursuit without effective preparation is a journey to frustration. Time spent in preparation is therefore time invested not wasted.

Every great business ventures is preceded by a dutiful preparation. The more detailed your preparation, the more distinguished is your result.

Zig Ziglar said, **'success occurs when opportunity meets preparation'. He also adds that a spectacular preparation precedes spectacular performance.**

Preparation will refine your talent as gold, it will increase your ability to prosper and be productive in all that you do. For you to succeed greatly in business, you must keep developing and maximizing your talent through effective preparation.

Even if your current level has brought you a measure of success in business, you must not rest on your oars, it is not your gift that makes you a success; it's preparing yourself for opportunities to use them. Henry Ford attributes the major reason for his business success to preparation, or ready. "Before everything else, getting ready is the secret of success".

Calvin Klein top fashion designer once said; "possibilities always exist. It's always out there if you really want it, and have the talent and you are prepared for the hard work. Then any new designer can achieve something far greater than I have achieved or Ralph Lauren or anyone else".

MAXIMUM EFFECTIVENESS

To ensure maximum effectiveness and the fullest realization of your vision, You must commit yourself to the necessary preparation.

Because preparation attracts opportunity, you cannot be over-prepared, you are more likely to be severely under prepared. And inadequate preparation produces inadequate result. we are largely victims of our lack of preparation. Thomas Edison said, "good fortune is what happens when opportunity meets with preparation".

Every business is at the mercy of preparation. Because you cannot get frustrated with facts. If you are trying to get ready when you are supposed to be ready, you are late.

FACT FINDING

Effective preparation is appropriate arrangement of facts, if you don't do mental work, you will end up doing menial work.

In fact-finding, you identify what you have and what you don't have. You examine the manpower, the money and the time at hand and you go ahead to make wise use of all you have at hand.

If you prepare very well for success in business and take practical steps toward implementation there is no way you will not succeed.

3

BE ADDICTED TO ACQUIRING RELEVANT INFORMATION

Today, knowledge has power. It controls access to opportunity and advancement.
– Peter Drucker

We live in a world of information. A world where having the right information matter a great deal. In today's world, information will make the difference between your present state and your future.

Great accomplishment in life and business answers to knowledge. The baseline for super achievements in your business is knowledge. The more you know the more capacity for success you develop. Your ability for great success in business is largely determined by the knowledge you are expose to. However, not only the exposure, but the application of the knowledge is also crucial.

So, the extra ordinary mind you possess brings result in business. I think I should let you know at this junction that success in business world of today is not just having a great idea alone but mentality as well. This is because without updating, there will be outdating. If you don't want your business to be outdated, keep updating.

Friend, you don't celebrate talent, you are only exalted by knowledge. If people behind you and your competitors happen to know better than you do, then you are retired from your leadership position, because a leader is a man doing great things.

It is your mental capacity that determines the size of your result. The difference between successful business people and failures is in what they know and also in what they do with what they know.

21ST CENTURY BUSINESS

Ignorance incapacitates, it can limit a man's business. If you do not learn anything new today; tomorrow will be no different. Be willing to go for every bit of information that can enhance and maximize your business, and you will be launched into greater things in business.

Leaders are learners. Strategic information is the key to the 21st century business. To succeed and excel in this fast changing business world of today, you will have to continually upgrade your knowledge and insight at a very fast pace.

"As a general rule the most successful man in life

is the man who has the best information" – Benjamin Disreali

MEET THE MOST RECOGNIZABLE ENTREPRENEUR IN THE U.K

Every successful business person in the world today encountered one information or the other, that brought about his business success.

Richard Branson, business mogul and billionaire founder of Virgin Airlines and Virgin Coke was rated the eleventh wealthiest Briton some years ago. He rose to the position by the information he came across from reading a little book.

"Small is beautiful"

Branson dropped out of school at the age of 19 and started business as a newspaper vendor. But the information he contacted from that little book paved the way for his great height in business. I read in a book how bankers threatened and saying they were not going to honour a £25 cheque that he issued.

Well, the story has changed today. Sir, Richard Branson is the most recognizable entrepreneur in the U.K.

Branson's conglomerate the virgin group employs over 7,500 people worldwide. About twenty of his managing directors and presidents have become millionaires today. He is the founder and chairman of Virgin Atlantic Airlines, Virgin Books, Virgin Bride, Virgin Mobile, Virgin Direct (insurance and pension scheme), Virgin Hotels, Virgin Island, Virgin Record, Virgin Trains, Virgin Cola and a Total of close to 200 companies.

MARY KAY'S SECRET

A man by the name of Glenn Bland was looking around the bookshop in an airport one day and he saw a book about wealth creation. In the book, the author claim to have studied the lives of over 500 millionaires and that the same practical steps it takes for anyone to break out of poverty into unimaginable wealth was clearly outlined in that book. Bland held tight to the book, "think and grow rich" by Napoleon Hill, bought and read it all through his journey on the plane.

He went a step further to believe the book and vowed he was going to obey the clear, practical steps to wealth outlined in it. Bland also gave himself a goal of starting an insurance company and growing it to be the most successful in America within five years.

He reached his goal and exceeded it. He became a multi-millionaire and philanthropist sponsoring many positive organisation and churches.

Another man by the name of A.L. Williams got hold of the same book, read and believed it, and went ahead to create a special market strategy. He started a business in life insurance, reached and exceeded his goal and his company had a turnover of $89 billion.

May Kay Ash was a lady who got a copy of this same book, read it and started her own business selling women's cosmetics. She is one of the most famous business women on earth.

She is worth over $2 billion dollars and her business is over $100 billion. Through the reading of the book, she was able to set up a marketing scheme for her products and today, Mary Kay's voice is the most powerful female voice in business. She has over 700,000 women selling

Mary Kay's cosmetics all over the world.

HOW TO GENERATE BUSINESS IDEA

Every committed reader will never lack ideas to succeed in business and a winning idea is the starting point of all riches. Books are a collection of facts, information, ideas and figures. When a man commit himself to acquiring relevant information in the area of his business, he will be opened to a world of ideas which will ultimately lead to creation of timely products and services. Then success will embrace him.

THREE WAYS OF ACQUIRING INFORMATION

1. **Reading**

Every Business Guru is a celebrated reader.

A man who does not read does not have an advantage over a man who cannot read. Many successful people in our world today are committed readers.

The secret of men is in their stories. The secrets of how some celebrated business people overcame the various challenges and obstacles that confronted them in the past can be found in books, magazines and business journals.

You have countless information represented by biographies and autobiographies of successful business people. Many years of experience can be transmitted through one book. Books contain solutions to difficulties.

Books offer you a great opportunity to relate with successful business people. There are many great business people who have achieved more than you in business. You can improve the quality of your life and business by relating with such people through their books.

2. **Listen to educative and informative audio programs**

As you listen to audio programme, you learn the message, you acquire the information, you tap into the knowledge content and you also receive great insights.

Many people have become millionaires through the miracle of listen CDS.

You can become one of the most successful business people just by listening to educational and informative audio CDS by experts.

"Soaking-in "audio CDS of great business people is an invaluable way of acquiring information and investing time. The time you spend listening to an audio CD programme is spent fellowshipping with the Guru. What a great privilege it is to interact with great mind for two hours in the privacy of your home.

Listen to audio programme also connects you to free consultancy. There are people in every area of human endeavour, who are deep enough to help.

These consultants are men who have great results in their areas of business specialization. For instance, who can be a better consultant on business success than Brian Tracy, America's leading authority on the development of human potential and personal effectiveness. The author of 100 absolutely unbreakable laws of business success and other best selling books. He is a dynamic and a successful businessman in every standard. He addresses more than 300,000 people each year on the subjects of personal, Professional and business success, including fortunes 500 companies and every size of business.

You may never be able to fix an appointment with him to see him but his audio and video learning programs are all around, to show you strategies and technicalities of business success.

3. **Attending seminars and educational business workshop**

The third key of acquiring knowledge is to attend every course and seminar you can possibly find that can help you to be a better business executive. Participate in education business programs.

The combination of reading books, listening to audio programs and attending business seminar will help you to move forward faster and accomplish great things in business.

4

PERSONAL RESPONSIBILITY

Hold yourself responsible for a higher standard than anybody else expects of you. Never excuse yourself.

– Henry Beecher

Personal responsibility is a state of been reliable, dependable and accountable, answerable and trust worth. You are where you are because of yourself, no one else.

The fact about responsibility is that for you to be successful and happy, responsibility is not optional; it is mandatory. Greater progress and accomplishment in your life and business is possible only to the degree to which you accept a higher level of responsibility. No one else can or will run your business for you. Personal responsibility is the price for greatness.

When you give your time and attention to your business, then you are on your way to experience extra ordinary breakthrough. All successful business people are responsible people. They don't blame circumstances, conditions or people for their failure in business. They have no excuses; they believe that their business success or failure is up to them.

Arthur Rubinstein, the great pianist, capsulated this principle of personal responsibility when he remarked that should he fail to practice one day, he would know it; should he skip practice for two days, the critics would know it; but should that extended to three days, the whole world will now it. A part-time church pianist might get way with a bit of a let down, but not an international acclaimed musician. Because more is required of him professionally.

7 KEYS TO PERSONAL RESPONSIBILITY

1. Refuse and resist any form of distraction to your assignment. Focus on your business and avoid unnecessary distraction.
2. Severe and separate any tie or relationship that is not connected to your assignment.
3. Constantly re-build your schedule, duties and the context of you assignment. Always set goals.
4. Be current with new development and innovation related to your assignment.
5. Be accountable to whatever fund or material that passes through you.
6. Win the trust and the confidence of your staff & customers.
7. Don't use people, manage them, be a manager of resources.

5

PERSONAL DEVELOPMENT

We must become the change we seek in the world

– Gandhi

Development means growing up gradually. It means becoming larger, mature, advanced or organized. It is through personal development you can maximize your business potential, stagnancy stinks.

Personal development is important to attain your business dream because you can only increase your reward, when you increase your value. The reason why you have to continuously developing yourself is because your growth is what determines who you are and who you are determines who you attract which consequently determines the success of your organization. No matter how talented you are, there is a place for growth and development.

BE A SUPER ACHIEVER

Great Achievers are men that constantly strive for excellence and improvement. They are never tired of striving for the best. The market is too jam-packed. So, for you to be outstanding, you must constantly develop yourself. Zig Ziglar said, "To be doing the same thing the same way and expecting to get a different result is the definition of insanity.

People will pay excellent rewards only for excellent work. You are therefore successful to the degree to which you do more things better than the average person.

Your talent is your gift or ability in its raw form. Unless it is developed or refined you can't get the best out of your gift. It is personal development that will refine your talent as gold. Personal development will increase your ability to prosper and be productive in all that you do.

NEW WAYS

Keep learning, keep leading and keep earning. Reading an hour a day in the area of your business will make you an authority in that field in the next two or three years.

For you to succeed in business, you must keep developing your skill and talent through learning.

Even if your current skills have brought you a

measure of success in life, you must still look for new ways of improving yourself.

Don't work on your business, work on yourself, and put all your effort into becoming a better person. Learn the skill practiced by successful business people and you will attract the kind of success they also enjoyed.

For you to survive, thrive and succeed in a fast changing world, you have to get back to the drawing board of learning. You will have to study and learn aggressively just to stay even and much more to get ahead because this is digital age and everything is fast changing.

Brian Tracy "one of America leading authorities on the development of human potential and personal effectiveness said something in one of his books that always amuse me. He said,

"if you are not continually learning and

upgrading your knowledge and skills, somewhere, someone is, and when you meet that person, you will lose".

MENTAL DEVELOPMENT

It is paramount that the mental capacity of every business owner must be developed. You must be well informed. You must know enough about your job. As a business executive, have relevant knowledge and information in regards to your business. One insight, small detail or winning idea can be the turning point in your business.

You must constantly search for how you can make your good better and your better best. See every problem that confronts you as an opportunity for mental development. Settle down to think it through.

Every problem you solve is a boost to your mental prowess. Remember, most development come through exercise. How well you live in riches and wealth is determined by how well your thoughts are channeled towards the direction of the problems you solve, the need you meet and the service you render, which will eventually generate wealth for you.

Bill Gates and Michael Dell solved problems in the area of computer technology and have made tons of money for themselves.

LIVE HEALTHY

The healthier you are, the smarter you live and the smarter you live the brighter you become. You need good health to command great result because when health is at stake, every other thing is grounded. There is no cure for carelessness. For a businessman to be at the cutting edge state till old age; the body must be given adequate care.

Seek professional counsel for the kind of food suitable for your body. If you want to endure in the race, don't overdrive yourself. occasional exercise under supervision can prove valuable. you need good health to be successful.

WORK ON YOUR APPEARANCE

A business owner is the best PRO of his business. He is the image maker (or destroyer) of what he stands for. People will pass verdict on your work based on how they see you appear. If you want to be successful, you need to dress like a successful person. Winners have image.

People see us before they hear us. What they see may quite prevent them from wanting to do business with you.

Use the top people in your area of business as models. Dress for where you are going to, not where you are coming from. Everyday is special.

6

HANDLING BUSINESS PRESSURE

Difficulties are opportunities to better things; they are stepping stones to greater experiences. Perhaps someday you will be thankful for some temporary failure in a particular direction. When a door closes, another always open as a natural law. It has to, to balance.   – Brian Adam

It does not take a scientist to know that everything that runs or flies, from cars to airplane is as powerful as the pressure generated in its engine. Yes, all progress and speed are functions of pressure.

Water appears to be the most 'gentle' element God ever created. But put it under pressure and it will give you all the electric energy to accomplish any wonder imaginable.

Friend, you need to learn to handle business pressure to become the wonder of your generation.

Business has never been for the "lily-livered". Progress is not for those who hate pressure.

No pressure, no progress!

"The great men who have lifted the world to higher levels were not developed in easy circumstances, but were rocked in the cradle of difficulties and pillowed in hardship. – Napoleon Hill.

GREAT OPPORTUNITIES INSIDE OPPOSITION

Without opposition in life and business, we generally misuse opportunities. So opportunities are maximized by oppositions. There is a price tag for every business achievements in life. For every journey that will lead to outstanding business success, opposition is inevitable. Opposition cannot be ruled out in your quest for success in life and business.

Opposition may come in form of criticisms, rejections, delay of rights, false accusation, hatred and so on. Business partners may become adversaries and friends may turn enemies, but you must become a master over opposition.

Every precious thing is a product of a determined

pressure. Pressure is one of the devices which force you to expand and be strong. There is probably no experience that could bring success which does not call for pressure in order to survive, thrive and excel.

STRATEGIES IN HANDLING BUSINESS PRESSURE

1. **Expect It**

This may look anti-faith on the surface, but it is not. It is learning to face reality. If you already know opposition will come, you won't be unnecessarily apprehensive when they show up.

Pressure is part of the business lifestyle. Expect it and rejoice in it as you grow into the status of a mighty business magnate.

2. **Before You Start Business Build Enough Stamina**

The wise man say: if you faint in the day of adversity, your strength is small. No one goes to war to learn how to operate the weapon.

3. **Learn to discern which opposition to neglect or dismiss and which one to act upon.** These will help you to conserve time.

4. **Don't dwell on the pain of opposition.** Rather focus on the joy of accomplishment.

5. **Always employ wisdom.**

When you resolve an opposition you end up with blessing.

6. **Make prayer your official way of responding to every opposition.**

    Nehemiah converted every trouble to a prayer point. He has the last laugh. Don't lose your position because of opposition. The opposition you see today may become your up-position tomorrow.

7. **Be on the move.**

    Opposition will always respect motion. It is not enough to be forward looking, you must also be forward moving.

7

COMMITMENT TO DUTY

The moment one definitely commit oneself, then providence moves too. All sorts of things occur to help one that would never otherwise have occurred.

– William Murray

Every success story in life and business is traceable to a dogged commitment. A chicken and a pig were having a discussion. The chicken said, "I am committed to giving one egg every day". That's not commitment, the pig said, "that is just participation; giving bacon, now that's commitment.

Martin Luther the King Jnr said, **"Until you are ready to die for a course, you are not fit to live".** Commitment to duties is very important to where you want to go in life.

Necessity is the mother of invention, when you begin to function under the law of necessity, you are on your way to hyper creativity.

Every truly committed person will be creative

Every creative person will be productive and

Every productive person will be successful.

Therefore the strong foundation for outstanding success in business is commitment to purpose.

Proverbs 22:29 says,"seest thou a man diligent in his business? He shall stand before kings; he shall not stand with mean men."

Where you sit tomorrow is determined by the

quality of your commitment to your task today. Your business success is not determined by connection, it is determined by your commitment to your business.

Jesus said in John 9:4 "I must work the works of him that sent me, while it is day: the night cometh, when no man can work'.

"He who would eat the fruit must climb the tree". – Scottish Proverb

Hard work is God's ancient principle to make your business a reality. No lazy person will ever experience true success in business! It takes hard work to fulfill your purpose and to accomplish greatness in this life. Be willing to invest your time and energy in your vision.

BE ON MOTION

Movement is the characteristics of every living thing and when you stop moving, you stop living. To stay in motion is to stay out of frustration in business. Only men in motion command distinction.

Opposition and obstacles will always respect motion. It is not enough to be forward looking, you must also be forward moving. Show me a man always in motion, you will soon find him on a mountain top. Just make sure you are taking steps and your vision will soon become a reality.

You don't discover new market until you have lost the sight of old ones. Business life is an adventure and only a committed explorer makes use of it. Only new steps guarantee new results.

Isaac Newton is still being celebrated today because he was a diligent worker. A plague had broken out in his school and all the students were asked to go home. Newton returned to his father's farm and did something useful with the eighteen month break.

It was during that period that he made those three outstanding discovering of the law of mechanics. Perhaps some of his mates whiled away their time, but Newton engaged the force of hard work.

I understand that the president of Daewoo Corporation, Kim Woo Chong works about 16 hours a stretch! He started his business about 30 years ago, and by 1977, his annual turn over was about $90 billion far above coca-cola and Rank Xerox! Hear his testimony.

"About seven years I started my own business 'worked for a company by a distant relative. Although I was part of the family, I was still a regular earner. Yet I did my work as though I was the owner of the company I did not wait for others, I always took the initiatives myself to seek out work to do. I was never late for work and never took a day off because of the inexpressible joy I derive from accomplishment. I still work as hard today."

Ordinary people with commitment can make an extraordinary impact on their world. John Maxwell.

8

DEVELOP YOUR MIND POWER

> **Thought is the original source of all wealth, all success, all material gain, all great discoveries and inventions, and of all achievement.** — **Cloube Bristol**

As far as your financial destiny is concerned, your mind is one of your greatest assets. Because the money you don't see with your mind, you can't touch with your hands. Every business breakthrough is traceable to breakthrough in the mind. This is a major fact your must grab.

There is a great power in your mind. You can

cause things to happen just by engaging your mental system. You can change your circumstances and experience by using your mind effectively.

BE AN ACHIEVER

I read the story of Bill Gates some years ago, when he was twelve years old, his mother was looking for him, Billy where are you, yelled his mum, suddenly he came out from one corner of the house and said,

"Mum, I am thinking don't you think".

No wonder, he became the richest man in the world. Friend, if Bill Gates can think his way to stardom, you can do it.

Ben Carson, a neurosurgeon, once said,

"Every human brain has more than fourteen billions cells and connection in human brain".

That's why your mind is one of the greatest assets God has given you to produce the breakthrough you desire in business.

You must breakthrough inside first before you breakthrough outside. If you experience breakthrough that cannot be traceable to your mind, you will lose it because your mind is the seat of business expansion.

THINK SOLUTION

The difference between producer and a consumer is their mind. Every testimony of business breakthrough in this world is a testimony of someone's mind.

Aeroplane – The Wright Brothers

Electricity – Michael Faraday

Bulb – Thomas Edison

Automobile – Henry Ford

Computer Charles Babbage

Microsoft – Bill Gates

Electric Motor – Joseph Henry

Electronics – Ambrose Fleming

There is a treasure on your inside that can profer solution to the problems of mankind.

You have a mind that can produce solution you are confronted with. Enough of physical sweat, mental sweat gives better result. Therefore think possibilities, think solution. Because you cannot think obstacles and get miracles, you cannot think problem and get solution'

Develop your mental power. You cannot think impossibilities and experience possibilities of the mind can conceive it, then it can achieve it.

Friend, the complexity is in your mind. People with scarcity mentality will suffer in the midst of plenty. The fact is that business is not as difficult as you think it is.

NOT YOUR COLOUR

It is not your size, colour, height or nation that makes your life and business colourful and valuable. It is your sound mind that distinguishes your life because a man that lost his common sense has lost his value.

Business starts from inside. True success is not what you have but who you are and your mindset. Therefore build your success from inside. Your business prosperity and progress will only be to the degree you prosper in your mind.

THINK BIG

The Bible says in **Luke 14:28, "for which of you, intending to build a tower, sitteth not down first, and counteth the cost, whether he have sufficient to finish it?**

Every tower builder is a tower thinker. If you must succeed in your business venture, you must be a great thinker because everything you see in the outside begins on the inside.

It is the depth of your thought that will determine the height of your business tower. Begin to assess where you are, assess where you want to be and program yourself to get there.

The story of the Wright Brothers, the inventors of the first airplane, is one that come to mind here. They simply had a open mind while all others had theirs tightly shut up. Everybody then thought it was impossible for a metal object to fly. Even clergymen criticized and labeled it an abominable imagination for man to think of flying! But the same clergyman later boarded the aircraft they once criticized.

Dear reader, keep an open mind today consider issues from all sides, not just some sides.

> *"Shallow mind believe in luck, but great minds believe in cause and effect". –*

Ralph Emerson.

Your mind is the operating factor, the fuel that drives your business to success. Because there is nothing you can do without first conceiving it in the mind and there' nothing you would do that would not first originate from the mind. Your mind is the greatest ingredient as a business executive to move forward. A business executive with an ineffective mind will lead a company or an organization to failure. The need to develop your mind power cannot be overemphasized in the life of an entrepreneur.

9

STRESS MANAGEMENT

The key to happiness is a sound mind in a sound body.

– Theodore Roosevelt

Stress can be defined as any interference that disturbs a person's health, mental and physical well being. It occurs when the body is required to perform beyond its normal range of capabilities.

The result of stress is harmful to individuals, families, businesses, society and organizations.

Stress has been called "the invisible disease", it is a disease that may affect you, your business, and any of the people working with you. So, you cannot afford to ignore it.

Though stress is a mind problem, if unchecked it will begin to infest and affect every area of our lives through inability to concentrate, irritability, anxiety, mental and emotional fatigue, boredom, apathy, uncontrolled appetite, e.t.c. Eventually it begins to affect the physical body organs like the heart; resulting in symptoms such as increase pounding, blood pressure, paralyses, up stomach, increased perspiration, nervous breakdown, headaches, eye tension, stammering, lack of stamina and tiredness. It begins to encroach on behavioral patterns – like, short temper, withdraw, isolation, increase and decreased appetite and libido, etch.

If unchecked still it result in condition such as ulcers, hypertension and psychological disorders. And if care is not taken it could degenerate into permanent mental disability.

Stress can ruin a promising business ventures, homes and families. The high rate of divorce rates in our world is due partly to the rapid increase in stress both at home and in the workplace.

Stress can be a business killer.

PRINCIPLE GUARANTEEING A STRESS-FREE LIFE

1. The Law Of Devotion

"But they that wait on the lord shall renew their strength...." Isa 40:31

Learn to wait on God than you run around for business activities. The more time you spend with God, the stronger and more energetic you become. The law of devotion helps you to keep your energy level emotionally, mentally and physically strong.

Spend more time in prayer and in the word of God. It is possible to be running around for business until you become a victim of expiration.

2. **The Law of Sabbath**

The Sabbath of rest is a perpetual principle. One of the most powerful keys to handling stress is; understanding the law of Sabbath.

The law of Sabbath means create time to rest.

There is a time to work and there is a time to rest.

When the body is denied adequate rest, it will soon begin to show signs of strain & stress. Stop overdriving yourself. Don't overdrive your staff.

3. **The Law of Delegation**

You can be doing other man's job until you lose

your own job. Delegation is getting someone capable. Look out for able men. And if you want able men, you must be willing to pay good wages. If you can only pay peasants all you can hire is a monkey. Don't only look for men who are gifted but also look out for men who know their job.

10

BUILD A BUSINESS TEAM ALLIANCE

Individual don't win; teams do. – Sam Waltons

One of the most critical factors of achieving business success is to build a business team alliance. It is a very powerful way to support your vision and bring unlimited resources to your business and personal life.

WHAT IS A BUSINESS TEAM ALLIANCE?

A business team alliance is a group of two or more individuals who voluntarily come together to creatively put their energy and resources together to accomplish some common goals.

Business team alliance is crucial to your success in business, with the business team alliance, you benefit from the other members who empower you and draw out your full potentials, mental resources and abilities. They trigger you, stimulate you to become all that you want to become.

Before Jesus started his ministry, he first recruited disciples. In business life, you cannot be totally successful alone. You need other people to inspire you, support you, encourage you and empower you to fulfill your purpose in life.

INVOLVE OTHERS

No dream is achieved in a vacuum, we all need the guidance and support that comes only from involving others. You must surround yourself with good people who posses solid experience. Don't try to build alone. Take your promising dream to people you trust and let them help you with their perspective and resources.

You must recognize that only God sends good quality people. Therefore every man you are bringing on board must be tested and proved before joining your team. You must cross-check before putting any man around you because your choice of men either make or break your dream. you cannot have Jonah on your boat and arrive safely at your own destination. Take time to study people around you before you place them.

Also, there must be a concrete agreement between

you and those working with you.

Make sure you are working based on facts.

J. Paul Getty, when asked what was the most important quality for a successful executive, replied, "It doesn't make much difference how much other knowledge or experience an executive possesses; if he is unable to achieve results through people, he is worthless, as an executive.

BENEFITS OF BUILDING A TEAM ALLIANCE

1. Results are multiplied than the sum of production of individual. Two are better than one for they have good results for their labour.
2. There is a better chance of accuracy of decision. Because in the multitude of counsel, there is safety.

3. It provide for mental, psychological, and emotional protection for team members.
4. It decreases the loneliness of leadership.
5. It increase the authority of the business leader with the people working with them. It increase people's confidence in leadership.
6. It enables friendship to develop, meeting team members social need.
7. It releases the talent and strengths of the team members and reduces frustration and failure in business.
8. It allow for mentoring of the team members by more experienced ones. Experience is the mother milk of a successful vision. The benefit of involving others in your vision is your instant accessibility to experience, progress, knowledge and wisdom.

HOW TO MAKE A BUSINESS TEAM ALLIANCE WORK

1. **Commitment**

    Commitment is the decision and willingness to pay the price to achieve the business objectives. As a business owner, you must know that commitment is not the same thing as involvement. Commitment is sacrifice. People that give excuses are not committed.

2. **Flexibility**

    Flexibility means willingness to change. As an entrepreneur, you have to be willing to yield and bend at times.

    Business life is about negotiation. Blessed are the flexible, for they shall not be bend out of shape.

    Rigidity and team alliance don't work together.

3. **Co-operative**

    You cannot be a team and still be working separately, you are in team to co-operate and not to compete.

4. **Communication and openness**

    This is essentially the oil in team work. What you have to say is as important as the way you say it. Work hard at understanding others. Try & develop listening skill.

5. **Humility**

    You have to humble yourself as a team player. Humility helps us to keep our head in shape.

6. **Discipline**

    Ability to conquer yourself. You need to control your appetite. Integrity is everything.

7. **Excellence**

    The quality of the team cannot be better than the team members. Excellence does not cost, it pays.

8. **Learn to work with the overall picture. Work with your vision in mind.**

9. **Faith**

    Team members must be optimistic. They must believe in the team objectives.

10. **Relational**

    You must relate and give respect to each others. Because we were created for connection.

No matter what kind of business you own, motivating your employees through effective relationship is very important.

OTHER BOOKS BY ISAAC GIWA.

1. Million dollar generating habit
2. Digging your diamond mine
3. Your mind is a miracle
4. Be a super achiever
5. Provoking your harvest
6. Seizing the moment
7. Secrets of financial success
8. Changing your world
9. Get ready...money cometh
10. Secrets for business success
11. Simple ideas on how to create your own miracle
12. Changing impossible situation
13. The secrets of highly successful people

14. 5 great ways to succeed in your own business
15. How to receive instance answer to your prayer
16. Becoming a proof producer
17. Be a success superstar
18. How to guarantee your success 100%
19. War against marital delay
20. War against wickedness
21. 12 rules for total life prosperity
22. Success handbook for single ladies
23. The business success principle
24. Success handbook for single men
25. The healing book
26. Success handbook for every woman
27. Deliverance handbook
28. Success in the market place
29. Fast track your career

30. Overcoming financial hardship

31. Secrets of dream interpretation

32. Decoding bad dreams (vol.1)

33. Decoding bad dreams (vol.2)

34. Dangerous prayers against bad (vol.1)

35. Dangerous prayers against bad dreams (vol.2)

36. Academic success

37. Success in the workplace

38. Successful single life

39. Wisdom for financial overflow

40. Fulfilling your destiny

41. 17 rules for great success

42. Overcoming anti-marriage forces

43. How to stay healthy

44. Praying for your children

45. Supernatural conception & childbirth

46. Money power

47. Success power

48. Essential ministers manual

49. Successful ministers manual

50. Achieving excellence in life & ministry

51. Mega impact

52. Wisdom for 21st century minister

53. Becoming an effective minister

54. 10 steps to fulfilling your ministry

55. Overcoming sexual bondage

56. Praying for your husband

57. Family deliverance prayer

58. Success handbook for everyman

59. Achieving career success

60. Success strategies for teens

61. Achievement secrets 101
62. How to achieve financial freedom
63. How to build a successful relationship
64. Failure is not final
65. Simple ways to get answers to your prayer
66. Start with nothing & achieve great success
67. Successful businessmen handbook
68. How to make your business work
69. Business success strategy that works
70. Business breakthrough ideas
71. Achieving outstanding business success
72. How to start & build your own business
73. Financial freedom for every woman
74. Wisdom
75. What every singles needs to know

76. The business woman's handbook
77. Wisdom for single ladies
78. How to be a successful female entrepreneur
79. Great rules for women in the work place
80. Career success for today's woman
81. How to start & profit with your own idea
82. A successful woman handbook
83. Woman power
84. How to be rich
85. Destiny secret 101
86. Maximizing your single life
87. The woman God uses
88. Start now...get rich
89. A woman's guide to miraculous conception
90. Dream power
91. Youth with a difference

92. Great rules for teenagers

93. Life skills for teens

94. In pursuit of destiny

95. 22 secrets of highly successful student.

GET CONNECTED

God is our power source.

He is the well-spring of wisdom. Once He comes into your heart a profound relationship with wisdom and power becomes inevitable. He is the foundation of grace. Without the flow of his divine grace, we malfunction and life becomes tedious. His graceful support is still available for you today.

He wants to help you in achieving your dreams and desires in life. He has helped many others. He can help you. So, my friends you too can enjoy his remarkable support today!

All you need to do is to accept Him as your Lord and Saviour. You will experience a change in your heart.

Say this prayer with me right now:

> **"Lord Jesus, thank you for dying for me on the cross". I turn to you to establish a relationship with you today. I ask that you forgive me my sins and cleanse me with your**

previous blood.

Let your life, grace and wisdom begin to find fulfillment. In my life today. Rule in my heart today as my Lord and personal Saviour.

Thank you for saving me.

OUR MISSION

- To let you know that God wants you to prosper and succeed.

- To help you discover the tremendous potential the creator has graciously invested in your life.

- To impact into your life the manifold wisdom of God.

- To ensure your total deliverance from failure and poverty.

- To release through effective prayer, the power of God to effect positive change in your circumstances.

YOUR LETTER IS VERY IMPORTANT TO ME

You are a special person to me and I believe that you are special to God.

I want to help you in any way possible. Do you have any prayer request? Write me when you need an intercessor to pray for you.

Let be hear from you when you are facing spiritual needs or experiencing a conflict in your business, marriage and career.

When you write, my staff and I will pray over your letter. I will write you back to help you receive the miracle you need.

I will look forward to your letter.

For more information, please contact;

ISAAC GIWA

Achieving Outstanding Business Success

Wisdom Impartation Ministries Int'l

P.O. box 621, Ikeja, Lagos-Nigeria.

Phone: 234-802-314-7715, 234-803-666-5662

E-Mail: wisdomimpart@yahoo.com

isaacgiwabooks@gmail..com

WILL YOU BECOME A PARTNER WITH MY MINISTRY?

Your Financial Seeds Are So Powerful In Helping Heal Broken Lives. When You Sow Into the Work of God, Miracle Harvest Are Guaranteed

*Supernatural protection. (Malachi 3:10)

*Supernatural favour (Luke 6:38)

*Supernatural Health (Isaiah (58:8)

*Supernatural wisdom & financial ideas. (Deuteronomy 8:18)

Sow your seed today, then focus your expectation for the 100 - fold return! An unusual seed will always create an unusual harvest.

To Sow Your Seed Today

Pay Into Any:

Bank: Guarantee Trust Bank

Account Name: Isaac Giwa

Account Number: 0006808883

Or Call,

+234-8023147715

+234-8036665662

+234-8189800366

E-Mail: wisdomimpart@yahoo.com

P.O. Box 621, Ikeja, Lagos, Nigeria.

BOOK ENCOUNTERS

A lot of people have received their breakthroughs just by reading Dr. Isaac Giwa's books. His books are life-changing manual and anointed spiritual weapons with which many fought battles over Failure, Stagnation, Poverty, Hardship, Afflictions e.t.c., and won!

Read these:

The book "Money Cometh" has done wonders to my finances. I recommend it for anyone that wants to succeed in this peculiar environment of Africa. It's a must read.

Olayinka Aina, Author:

Enjoy A Superb Service Year"

Lagos-Nigeria

Your book is an inspiring one and very intellectual. It has taught me how to be wise financially.

Josephine Asare, Author:

"All About Your Dreams

Accra-Ghana

I have read your book titled "secret of BUSINESS SUCCESS" I found the book quite educative, informative and above all it's a book that anybody that wants to succeed in business need to go through.

-Hassan Yusuf

Kaduna-Nigeria

Sir, the hunger and the burning to change my world have been eaten me up lately. Thank God for coming across your book "CHANGING YOUR WORLD" it's a booster.

Thanks.

-Michael A.

Lagos-Nigeria.

www.ingramcontent.com/pod-product-compliance
Lightning Source LLC
Chambersburg PA
CBHW020928180526
45163CB00007B/2924